WAGILE PROJECT MANAGEMENT :

BRIDGING THE GAP BETWEEN WATERFALL AND AGILE

Dedication

Sharvil,

who makes me realize
that parenting is a project and I will have to keep inventing and
executing
new methodologies to execute this lifetime project successfully.

Table of Content

Chapter 1: Understanding WAgile Project Management

Chapter 2: WAgile Project Lifecycle

Chapter 3: Integrating Waterfall and Agile Practices

Chapter 7: Iterative Development and Delivery

Chapter 8: Embracing Change and Continuous Improvement

Chapter 9: Monitoring and Controlling WAgile Projects

Chapter 10: Scaling WAgile for Large Projects and Organizations

Conclusion

Introduction

Welcome to the world of WAgile Project Management, a methodology that combines the best of both Waterfall and Agile approaches. In today's fast-paced business environment, organizations often face the challenge of balancing the need for structure and predictability with the flexibility and adaptability required to meet evolving customer demands. WAgile Project Management provides a solution by blending the strengths of Waterfall and Agile methodologies to drive successful project outcomes.

Chapter 1: Understanding WAgile Project Management

1.1 The Origins of WAgile:

The term "WAgile" is a combination of "Waterfall" and "Agile," reflecting the merging of these two project management methodologies. Waterfall, a traditional sequential approach, emphasizes upfront planning and defined phases, while Agile focuses on iterative development and adaptability. WAgile project management emerged as a response to the need for a flexible yet structured approach to project delivery.

1.2   Key Principles and Values:

WAgile project management incorporates key principles and values from both Waterfall and Agile methodologies. Some of the essential principles and values of WAgile include:

1.2.1 Structured Planning:

Borrowed from Waterfall, WAgile emphasizes detailed planning and requirements gathering at the beginning of the project. This provides a solid foundation for subsequent development iterations.

1.2.2 Iterative Development:

Drawing from Agile, WAgile promotes iterative development and delivery, allowing for feedback, adaptation, and continuous improvement throughout the project lifecycle.

1.2.3 Collaboration and Cross-Functional Teams:

WAgile emphasizes collaboration among team members and stakeholders, breaking down silos and fostering a culture of teamwork and shared responsibility.

1.2.4 Flexibility and Adaptability:

WAgile embraces the Agile value of responding to change over following a rigid plan. It allows for modifications to requirements and priorities based on evolving customer needs and market dynamics.

1.2.5 Continuous Improvement:

Similar to Agile, WAgile encourages a culture of continuous improvement through retrospectives, lessons learned, and implementing changes based on feedback.

1.3 Benefits and Challenges of WAgile:

Implementing WAgile project management can bring several benefits to organizations. These advantages include:

1.3.1 Flexibility and Adaptability:

By combining the structured approach of Waterfall with the flexibility of Agile, WAgile enables organizations to respond quickly to changing market conditions, customer feedback, and emerging requirements.

1.3.2 Improved Stakeholder Collaboration:

WAgile promotes close collaboration and involvement of stakeholders throughout the project, fostering better communication, shared understanding, and increased customer satisfaction.

1.3.3 Faster Time to Market:

The iterative nature of WAgile allows for early delivery of working increments, enabling organizations to release valuable features to customers sooner and gain a competitive advantage.

1.3.4 Enhanced Risk Management:

By incorporating regular feedback loops, WAgile enables early identification and mitigation of risks, reducing the chances of costly failures or delays.

Despite its advantages, WAgile project management also comes with its share of challenges, including:

a) Balancing Structure and Flexibility:

Striking the right balance between structure and flexibility can be challenging. Organizations must find the optimal level of planning and adaptability that suits their specific project requirements.

b) Change Management:

Embracing change is a core tenet of WAgile, but managing changes effectively requires a robust change management process to prevent scope creep and ensure alignment with project goals.

c) Team Collaboration:

Collaborating effectively within cross-functional teams and across different disciplines can be a challenge, particularly when teams are geographically dispersed or have conflicting priorities.

1.4   When to Use WAgile:

WAgile project management is suitable for a variety of scenarios, including:

1.4.1 Projects with Evolving Requirements:

When requirements are likely to change or evolve during the project, WAgile allows for flexibility in accommodating these changes.

1.4.2 Time-Sensitive Projects:

WAgile's iterative approach facilitates quicker delivery of working increments, making it well-suited for projects with tight deadlines or time-sensitive deliverables.

1.4.3 Cross-Functional Projects:

Projects that require collaboration and coordination across multiple departments or disciplines can benefit from the cross-functional team structure and collaborative nature of WAgile.

1.4.4 Projects with High Customer Interaction:

If frequent customer involvement and feedback are crucial for project success, WAgile provides a framework for continuous customer engagement and iteration.

Chapter 2: WAgile Project Lifecycle

2.1 Initiation and Project Definition:

The WAgile project lifecycle begins with project initiation and definition, where the project's purpose, goals, and objectives are clearly established. Key activities in this phase include:

2.1.1 Project Charter:

Creating a project charter that outlines the project's scope, objectives, stakeholders, and initial high-level plan.

2.1.2 Stakeholder Identification:

Identifying and engaging relevant stakeholders to ensure their involvement and support throughout the project.

2.1.3 Project Team Formation:

Forming a cross-functional project team with the necessary skills and expertise to execute the project successfully.

2.1.4 Project Scope Definition:

Clearly defining the boundaries and deliverables of the project, ensuring a shared understanding among the team and stakeholders.

2.2   Planning and Requirements Gathering:

In this phase, the project team focuses on detailed planning and requirements gathering. Key activities include:

2.2.1 Detailed Project Planning:

Developing a comprehensive project plan, including activities, timelines, resources, and dependencies. This plan provides a roadmap for the entire project.

2.2.2 Requirement Elicitation:

Engaging stakeholders to identify and document project requirements, ensuring that all expectations are captured and understood.

2.2.3 Requirements Prioritization:

Prioritizing requirements based on their business value, feasibility, and impact on project success. This helps in optimizing resource allocation and managing scope.

2.2.4 Work Breakdown Structure (WBS):

Creating a WBS to break down project tasks into manageable components, facilitating better planning, estimation, and tracking.

2.3   Iterative Development and Delivery:

The iterative development and delivery phase is at the core of the WAgile project lifecycle. It involves the following key activities:

2.3.1 Sprint Planning:

Defining the goals, scope, and tasks for each sprint or iteration. This involves breaking down requirements into actionable user stories and estimating effort.

2.3.2 Sprint Execution:

The project team works collaboratively to develop and deliver the functionality defined for the current sprint, following Agile principles and practices.

2.3.3 Daily Stand-up Meetings:

Conducting brief daily meetings to synchronize activities, discuss progress, address challenges, and ensure alignment within the team.

2.3.4 Incremental Delivery:

At the end of each sprint, a potentially shippable increment of the project is delivered, providing value to stakeholders and allowing for early feedback.

2.4   Continuous Feedback and Adaptation:

WAgile emphasizes continuous feedback and adaptation throughout the project lifecycle. Key activities in this phase include:

2.4.1 Sprint Review:

Conducting a review at the end of each sprint to demonstrate the delivered increment to stakeholders, gather feedback, and validate against the project's objectives.

2.4.2 Retrospective Meetings:

Holding retrospectives to reflect on the sprint and identify areas for improvement. This includes discussing what went well, what could be improved, and action items for the next sprint.

2.4.3 Change Management:

Effectively managing change requests and incorporating them into future sprints based on their prioritization and impact on project goals.

2.4.4 Continuous Improvement:

Encouraging the project team to implement process improvements and learn from past experiences, ensuring a culture of continuous learning and growth.

2.5 Project Closure and Evaluation:

The final phase of the WAgile project lifecycle involves project closure and evaluation. Key activities include:

2.5.1 Project Handover:

Transferring project deliverables, documentation, and knowledge to relevant stakeholders or operational teams as needed.

2.5.2 Project Evaluation:

Conducting a comprehensive assessment of the project's success against the defined objectives, including analyzing project performance, stakeholder satisfaction, and lessons learned.

2.5.3 Celebrating Successes and Recognizing Contributions:

Acknowledging the achievements and contributions of the project team members and stakeholders, fostering a positive project culture.

2.5.4 Post-Project Review:

Performing a post-project review to identify areas of improvement in the WAgile project management approach itself

Chapter 3:
Integrating Waterfall and Agile Practices

3.1   Waterfall Practices in WAgile:

3.1.1 Detailed Planning and Documentation:

WAgile incorporates the Waterfall practice of detailed planning and documentation to ensure a solid foundation for the project. This includes creating comprehensive project plans, defining requirements, and documenting project scope. The aim is to establish a clear roadmap and set expectations upfront.

However, in WAgile, the planning and documentation are adapted to be more flexible and iterative. Rather than creating extensive upfront documentation, WAgile focuses on creating "just enough" documentation that is necessary for the current stage or sprint. This allows for the inclusion of changes and adaptation as the project progresses.

3.1.2 Sequential Execution and Phases:

WAgile retains the concept of sequential execution and phased approach from Waterfall. It acknowledges that certain activities need to be completed in a specific order and that some dependencies exist.

However, unlike traditional Waterfall, WAgile projects work in shorter iterations or sprints within each phase. This allows for frequent feedback, integration, and validation, enabling early detection and resolution of issues. The phased approach helps to maintain a structured framework while allowing for flexibility and adaptation within each phase.

3.1.3 Predictive Decision-Making:

Waterfall projects rely on predictive decision-making, where decisions are made based on upfront planning and analysis. This approach assumes that all requirements and project details can be accurately determined at the beginning.

In WAgile, while the initial planning is still important, decision-making is more adaptive and based on feedback and data gathered during each iteration. The project team and stakeholders collaborate to make informed decisions based on the current project status, customer needs, and market dynamics. This allows for a more dynamic and responsive decision-making process.

3.2   Agile Practices in WAgile:

3.2.1 Iterative Development and Delivery:

WAgile incorporates the Agile practice of iterative development and delivery. The project is divided into short iterations or sprints, where working increments are developed, tested, and delivered. Each sprint focuses on delivering a set of prioritized requirements or user stories.

This iterative approach allows for early and frequent feedback from stakeholders, enabling the project team to make necessary adjustments and improvements throughout the project. It ensures that value is continuously delivered and reduces the risk of late-stage surprises or deviations from expectations.

3.2.2 Cross-Functional Teams and Collaboration:

Agile promotes cross-functional teams and collaboration, and WAgile follows this principle as well. In WAgile projects, teams are composed of individuals with diverse skills and expertise relevant to the project's requirements. This includes representatives from different functional areas such as development, design, testing, and business analysis.

Collaboration within the team and with stakeholders is encouraged throughout the project lifecycle. This promotes knowledge sharing, shared responsibility, and a holistic understanding of the project, leading to better decision-making and more effective problem-solving.

3.2.3 Embracing Change and Continuous Improvement:

Agile places a strong emphasis on embracing change and continuous improvement, and WAgile adopts this mindset as well. It recognizes that requirements and priorities may change over time, and it embraces the idea of responding to those changes.

WAgile encourages open communication, feedback loops, and regular retrospectives to identify areas for improvement. It creates an environment where team members are empowered to suggest changes, experiment with new ideas, and implement improvements continuously. This allows for adaptability and continuous learning throughout the project.

3.3   Balancing Structure and Flexibility:

WAgile project management embraces the delicate balance between structure and flexibility, acknowledging that both are crucial for success. By implementing a robust framework, WAgile enables thorough planning, seamless coordination, and efficient control over project activities. However, it also prioritizes flexibility, understanding that projects are prone to uncertainties and alterations. This adaptive approach empowers teams to respond swiftly to changing requirements, stakeholder inputs, and market dynamics, fostering innovation and delivering high-value outcomes. WAgile's emphasis on striking this equilibrium ensures projects stay on course while embracing the agility needed to thrive in a dynamic and ever-evolving business landscape.

Chapter 4: Managing Stakeholder Expectations

4.1 Identifying and Engaging Stakeholders:

Managing stakeholder expectations begins with identifying and engaging the relevant stakeholders. Stakeholders are individuals or groups who have an interest or influence in the project's outcome. Key activities include:

4.1.1 Stakeholder Analysis:

Conducting a stakeholder analysis to identify and categorize stakeholders based on their level of interest, influence, and impact on the project.

4.1.2 Stakeholder Mapping:

Creating a stakeholder map to visualize the relationships and interactions among stakeholders and determine the most effective strategies for engagement.

4.1.3 Stakeholder Engagement Plan:

Developing a stakeholder engagement plan that outlines the objectives, strategies, and communication channels for engaging with each stakeholder throughout the project.

4.2   Setting Realistic Expectations:

Setting realistic expectations is essential to ensure alignment between project outcomes and stakeholder needs. It involves:

4.2.1 Scope Definition:

Clearly defining the project scope, deliverables, and limitations to establish realistic boundaries and avoid scope creep.

4.2.2 Requirements Prioritization:

Collaboratively prioritizing project requirements with stakeholders to manage expectations regarding what will be delivered within the given time and resources.

4.2.3 Managing Constraints:

Communicating and managing constraints such as budget, timeline, and resource limitations, ensuring stakeholders understand the trade-offs and potential impacts on the project.

4.2.4 Managing Risks:

Proactively identifying and managing risks that may affect stakeholder expectations, communicating the mitigation strategies and potential impact on project outcomes.

4.3 Communication and Transparency:

Effective communication and transparency are vital for managing stakeholder expectations. Key considerations include:

4.3.1 Communication Plan:

Developing a communication plan that outlines the frequency, methods, and content of project updates, ensuring stakeholders are informed and involved.

4.3.2 Clear and Timely Information:

Providing stakeholders with clear, accurate, and timely information about the project's progress, milestones, challenges, and decisions.

4.3.3 Two-Way Communication:

Encouraging open and two-way communication, actively listening to stakeholders' concerns, feedback, and expectations, and addressing them in a timely manner.

4.3.4 Transparency:

Being transparent about project risks, issues, and changes, sharing relevant information openly to build trust and manage stakeholder expectations.

4.4   Stakeholder Involvement throughout the Project:

Involving stakeholders throughout the project lifecycle is crucial for managing their expectations effectively. This can be achieved through:

4.4.1 Stakeholder Engagement Strategy:

Developing an engagement strategy that outlines how stakeholders will be involved in decision-making, feedback collection, and validation activities.

4.4.2 Regular Updates and Reporting:

Providing regular project updates and progress reports to stakeholders, showcasing achievements, challenges, and the impact of their involvement.

4.4.3 Stakeholder Workshops and Reviews:

Conducting workshops and reviews where stakeholders can provide feedback, review deliverables, and participate in discussions to influence project outcomes.

4.4.4 Stakeholder Feedback Mechanisms:

Establishing feedback mechanisms such as surveys, interviews, or feedback sessions to gather stakeholder opinions and insights, ensuring their voices are heard and considered.

By implementing these strategies, project managers can effectively manage stakeholder expectations, foster a collaborative environment, and enhance stakeholder satisfaction throughout the project lifecycle.

Chapter 5:
Agile Planning in a WAgile Environment

5.1 Defining Project Goals and Objectives:

Agile planning in a WAgile environment begins with clearly defining project goals and objectives. This involves:

5.1.1 Project Vision:

Establishing a shared understanding of the project's purpose and desired outcomes among the project team and stakeholders.

5.1.2 SMART Goals:

Setting Specific, Measurable, Achievable, Relevant, and Time-bound (SMART) goals that align with the project vision. These goals serve as a guide for planning and decision-making throughout the project.

5.1.3 Key Success Criteria:

Identifying the key criteria that will determine the success of the project, such as customer satisfaction, product quality, or return on investment.

5.1.4 Stakeholder Alignment:

Ensuring that project goals and objectives are communicated and aligned with the expectations and needs of the stakeholders.

5.2   Agile Planning Techniques:

5.2.1 User Stories and Epics:

User stories and epics are key planning techniques in Agile. User stories capture the requirements from the user's perspective and describe the desired functionality or value. Epics, on the other hand, represent larger, more complex user stories that need to be broken down into smaller, manageable units.

Using user stories and epics allows the project team to focus on delivering value incrementally, enabling prioritization based on customer needs and feedback.

5.2.2 Agile Estimation and Sizing:

Agile planning involves estimation and sizing of user stories or tasks to determine the effort required for implementation. Agile teams use various techniques for estimation, such as Planning Poker, T-shirt sizing, or relative sizing (e.g., using story points).

Estimation provides a basis for prioritization, resource allocation, and release planning. It helps in managing stakeholder expectations by providing a better understanding of what can be achieved within a given time frame.

5.2.3 Release and Iteration Planning:

Agile planning includes release planning and iteration planning. Release planning involves determining the scope and timeline for delivering a set of features or functionalities. It considers the project's priorities, dependencies, and constraints to create a roadmap for incremental delivery.

Iteration planning focuses on planning the work to be done within a specific iteration or sprint. It involves selecting user stories from the product backlog, breaking them down into tasks, estimating effort, and assigning them to the team members.

Both release and iteration planning involve collaboration among the project team, stakeholders, and product owner to ensure alignment with project goals and stakeholder expectations.

5.3   Creating a Flexible Project Schedule:

In a WAgile environment, a flexible project schedule is essential to accommodate changing priorities and evolving requirements. This includes:

5.3.1 Timeboxing:

Using timeboxing techniques to allocate fixed time periods for specific activities, such as sprint duration or release cycles. This helps in maintaining a predictable and manageable project cadence.

5.3.2 Iterative and Incremental Delivery:

Breaking the project into iterative cycles or sprints to deliver increments of value at regular intervals. This allows for feedback, adaptation, and reprioritization, ensuring that the project remains aligned with stakeholder expectations.

5.3.3 Buffer Management:

Incorporating buffers or contingency time within the project schedule to account for uncertainties, risks, and unexpected changes. This provides flexibility to handle unforeseen events without compromising the project timeline.

5.3.4 Adaptive Planning:

Embracing the Agile principle of responding to change over following a rigid plan. This involves being open to adjusting the project schedule based on feedback, stakeholder needs, and market dynamics.

By adopting these Agile planning techniques and creating a flexible project schedule, project managers can effectively navigate uncertainties, manage stakeholder expectations, and ensure successful project outcomes in a WAgile environment.

Chapter 6:
Effective Collaboration and Cross-Functional Teams

6.1 Building and Managing Cross-Functional Teams:

Building and managing cross-functional teams is crucial for effective collaboration in a WAgile environment. Key considerations include:

6.1.1 Team Composition:

Assembling a diverse team with individuals possessing different skills, expertise, and perspectives relevant to the project's requirements. This ensures a well-rounded approach to problem-solving and decision-making.

6.1.2 Clear Roles and Responsibilities:

Defining clear roles and responsibilities for each team member, ensuring alignment with project goals and expectations. This clarity promotes accountability and efficient collaboration.

6.1.3 Team Development:

Nurturing team dynamics and fostering a culture of collaboration and trust. This includes team-building activities, promoting open communication, and providing opportunities for skill development and growth.

6.2 Facilitating Collaboration and Knowledge Sharing:

Effective collaboration and knowledge sharing are essential for the success of WAgile projects. Strategies for facilitating collaboration include:

6.2.1 Communication Channels:

Establishing appropriate communication channels, both synchronous and asynchronous, to enable team members to connect, share information, and collaborate effectively. This may include project management tools, instant messaging platforms, and collaboration software.

6.2.2 Collaborative Workspaces:

Creating physical or virtual spaces where team members can collaborate, share ideas, and work together on project deliverables. These spaces can facilitate brainstorming, information sharing, and collective decision-making.

6.2.3 Knowledge Management:

Implementing knowledge management practices to capture, organize, and share project-related knowledge and lessons learned. This ensures that valuable insights and best practices are documented and accessible to the team throughout the project.

6.3 Agile Leadership and Empowering Teams:

Agile leadership plays a critical role in promoting effective collaboration and empowering cross-functional teams. This involves:

6.3.1 Servant Leadership:

Adopting a servant leadership approach, where leaders support the team's needs, remove obstacles, and foster a collaborative and empowered work environment. Leaders serve as facilitators and enablers rather than traditional command-and-control managers.

6.3.2 Empowering Decision-Making:

Empowering teams to make decisions within their areas of expertise and influence. This encourages ownership, autonomy, and accountability, fostering a sense of ownership and commitment among team members.

6.3.3 Coaching and Mentoring:

Providing coaching and mentoring support to team members, helping them develop their skills, overcome challenges, and achieve their full potential. This includes providing guidance, feedback, and opportunities for skill enhancement.

6.4 Overcoming Challenges in Distributed Teams:

In today's globalized world, distributed teams are becoming increasingly common. Overcoming challenges in distributed teams requires specific considerations, such as:

6.4.1 Effective Communication:

Establishing clear communication channels and protocols to overcome geographical and time zone differences. Leveraging technology tools for video conferencing, virtual collaboration, and project management software can facilitate seamless communication.

6.4.2 Building Trust:

Fostering trust among team members, despite physical distance, by encouraging open and transparent communication, fostering a culture of collaboration, and creating opportunities for team bonding and relationship-building.

6.4.3 Collaboration Tools and Platforms:

Utilizing collaboration tools and platforms that enable remote team members to collaborate on shared documents, track progress, and facilitate real-time communication. This ensures everyone has access to the necessary information and promotes collaboration regardless of location.

6.4.4 Cultural Sensitivity:

Recognizing and respecting cultural differences within the team and adapting communication and collaboration approaches accordingly. This includes understanding different work styles, norms, and expectations to foster an inclusive and supportive environment.

By focusing on building and managing cross-functional teams, facilitating collaboration and knowledge sharing, promoting agile leadership, and addressing challenges in distributed teams, project managers can create an environment conducive to effective collaboration and ultimately enhance project success in a WAgile environment.

Chapter 7: Iterative Development and Delivery

7.1 Agile Development Practices in Wagile:

Agile development practices are a core component of Wagile project management. This chapter explores how these practices can be effectively integrated into the Wagile approach. Key practices include:

7.1.1 User Stories and Prioritization:

Breaking down project requirements into user stories and prioritizing them based on customer value, complexity, and dependencies. This allows for incremental delivery and ensures that the most valuable features are developed first.

7.1.2 Iterative Development:

Adopting iterative development cycles, such as sprints, to deliver working increments of the product at regular intervals. This approach allows for frequent feedback, continuous improvement, and adaptation based on stakeholder input.

7.1.3 Test-Driven Development (TDD):

Emphasizing the creation of automated tests before writing the code. TDD ensures that the developed software meets the defined requirements and maintains the desired quality throughout the development process.

7.1.4 Continuous Integration and Deployment:

Implementing practices that enable the integration of code changes from multiple team members on a regular basis. This promotes early detection of integration issues and enables the rapid deployment of new features or bug fixes.

7.2   Sprint Planning and Execution:

Sprint planning and execution are integral to iterative development in a WAgile environment. Key considerations include:

7.2.1 Sprint Planning:

Collaboratively selecting a set of user stories or tasks from the product backlog for the upcoming sprint. This involves estimating effort, breaking down stories into smaller tasks, and defining the sprint goal and deliverables.

7.2.2 Task Allocation:

Assigning tasks to team members based on their expertise and availability. Ensuring a balance of workload and fostering cross-functional collaboration.

7.2.3 Daily Stand-up Meetings:

Conducting daily stand-up meetings to provide a brief status update on progress, discuss any obstacles or dependencies, and coordinate efforts within the team.

7.2.4 Sprint Review and Retrospective:

Reviewing the completed work with stakeholders at the end of the sprint and gathering feedback. Conducting a retrospective to reflect on the sprint's successes, challenges, and areas for improvement.

7.3 Measuring Progress and Tracking Metrics:

Measuring progress and tracking relevant metrics is essential for monitoring project performance in an iterative development model. Key metrics to consider include:

7.3.1 Velocity:

Tracking the team's velocity, which measures the amount of work completed in each sprint. Velocity provides insights into the team's capacity and helps in forecasting project timelines and future iterations.

7.3.2 Burn-Down and Burn-Up Charts:

Using burn-down and burn-up charts to visualize the remaining work or completed work over time. These charts help in assessing progress, identifying potential bottlenecks, and making data-driven decisions.

7.3.3 Cycle Time:

Measuring the time taken for a user story or task to move through the development process, from initiation to completion. Cycle time highlights bottlenecks and process inefficiencies, enabling continuous improvement.

7.3.4 Customer Satisfaction:

Collecting feedback from stakeholders and end-users to assess their satisfaction with the delivered features and overall product quality. This feedback helps in refining priorities and enhancing the user experience.

7.4 Continuous Integration and Quality Assurance:

Continuous integration and quality assurance practices play a critical role in ensuring a high-quality product in a WAgile environment. Key practices include:

7.4.1 Automated Testing:

Implementing automated testing frameworks to perform unit tests, integration tests, and regression tests. Automated testing helps detect defects early and ensures the stability and reliability of the product.

7.4.2 Code Reviews:

Conducting peer code reviews to identify potential bugs, improve code quality, and ensure adherence to coding standards. Code reviews promote collaboration and knowledge sharing among team members.

7.4.3 Continuous Integration:

Integrating code changes from multiple developers into a shared repository on an ongoing basis. Continuous integration helps identify integration issues early and maintains the stability of the codebase.

Chapter 8: Embracing Change and Continuous Improvement

8.1 Adapting to Changing Requirements:

In a WAgile project management approach, the ability to adapt to changing requirements is crucial for success. This chapter explores strategies for embracing change effectively. Key considerations include:

8.1.1 Agile Mindset:

Cultivating an agile mindset among the project team and stakeholders, which values flexibility, embraces uncertainty, and views change as an opportunity for improvement rather than a hindrance.

8.1.2 Continuous Stakeholder Engagement:

Maintaining regular communication and collaboration with stakeholders to understand their evolving needs, gather feedback, and incorporate changes into the project plan.

8.1.3 Prioritization and Trade-offs:

Being prepared to reprioritize and make trade-offs when new requirements or changes arise. This involves assessing the impact on project scope, timeline, and resources and making informed decisions to accommodate the changes.

8.2   Agile Change Management Techniques:

Agile change management techniques provide a structured approach to managing and implementing changes in a WAgile environment. Key techniques include:

8.2.1 Change Backlog:

Creating a change backlog to capture and prioritize requested changes. Similar to the product backlog, the change backlog allows for transparency and informed decision-making.

8.2.2 Change Control Boards:

Establishing change control boards or committees comprising relevant stakeholders to review, evaluate, and approve proposed changes. These boards ensure that changes align with project objectives and minimize disruptions.

8.2.3 Iterative Planning and Adaptation:

Leveraging the iterative nature of WAgile to incorporate changes in upcoming iterations or sprints. This enables the project team to quickly respond to evolving requirements and deliver value in a timely manner.

8.3 Retrospectives and Lessons Learned:

Retrospectives and lessons learned sessions are essential for continuous improvement in a WAgile environment. Key practices include:

8.3.1 Sprint Retrospectives:

Conducting sprint retrospectives at the end of each iteration to reflect on what went well, what could be improved, and actionable items for the next iteration. This allows the team to make continuous adjustments and enhance their processes.

8.3.2 Lessons Learned Sessions:

Holding lessons learned sessions at key project milestones or at the end of the project to capture insights, best practices, and areas for improvement. This information can then be shared across the organization and applied to future projects.

8.3.3 Knowledge Sharing and Documentation:

Encouraging the documentation and sharing of lessons learned, best practices, and success stories to foster a learning culture within the project team and organization as a whole. This ensures that valuable knowledge is captured and can be leveraged in future projects.

8.4 Cultivating a Culture of Continuous Improvement:

Cultivating a culture of continuous improvement is essential for long-term success in a WAgile environment. Strategies for fostering this culture include:

8.4.1 Collaboration and Open Feedback:

Encouraging collaboration, open communication, and constructive feedback among team members. This creates an environment where ideas for improvement can be shared freely, and everyone feels empowered to contribute.

8.4.2 Encouraging Innovation:

Providing space and resources for experimentation, creativity, and innovation. This enables the team to explore new approaches, technologies, and techniques that can enhance project outcomes.

8.4.3 Learning and Development Opportunities:

Investing in training, workshops, and continuous learning opportunities for team members to enhance their skills and stay updated with industry best practices. This investment in professional growth contributes to the team's ability to drive continuous improvement.

8.4.4 Celebrating Successes:

Recognizing and celebrating project successes and achievements, both big and small. This fosters a positive and motivating environment, reinforcing the importance of continuous improvement and acknowledging the value of the team's efforts.

By embracing change, adopting agile change management techniques, conducting retrospectives, and cultivating a culture of continuous improvement, organizations can enhance their project management practices and drive success in a WAgile environment.

Chapter 9: Monitoring and Controlling WAgile Projects

9.1 Tracking Progress and Managing Risks:

Monitoring and controlling project progress and managing risks are crucial for successful project delivery in a WAgile environment. Key considerations include:

9.1.1 Agile Project Tracking:

Implementing tools and techniques to track the progress of project deliverables and tasks. This may include visual management boards, burndown charts, Kanban boards, or project management software that provide real-time visibility into project status.

9.1.2 Risk Identification and Mitigation:

Proactively identifying and assessing project risks and developing mitigation strategies. Regular risk reviews and risk management activities help minimize the impact of potential risks and maintain project momentum.

9.1.3 Issue Management:

Establishing a systematic approach to identify, track, and resolve project issues. Promptly addressing and resolving issues helps prevent them from escalating and impacting project progress.

9.2   Agile Project Metrics and Reporting:

Agile project metrics and reporting provide valuable insights into project performance and help stakeholders make informed decisions. Key metrics and reporting practices include:

9.2.1 Cycle Time:

Tracking the time taken for a user story or task to move through the development process. Cycle time metrics provide visibility into the efficiency of the team's workflow and highlight potential bottlenecks.

9.2.2 Lead Time:

Measuring the time from the initiation of a user story to its completion and delivery. Lead time metrics help assess the overall project speed and time-to-market.

9.2.3 Velocity and Burndown Charts:

Monitoring the team's velocity, which measures the amount of work completed in each iteration. Burndown charts visualize the remaining work or completed work over time, providing insights into project progress and forecasting.

9.2.4 Agile Dashboards:

Creating dashboards or visual representations of project metrics to provide a comprehensive overview of project performance. Dashboards may include metrics related to scope, schedule, budget, quality, and stakeholder satisfaction.

9.3 Addressing Scope Creep and Managing Expectations:

Scope creep, the uncontrolled expansion of project scope, can impact project success. Managing scope creep and setting realistic expectations are essential. Key strategies include:

9.3.1 Clear Project Definition:

Ensuring a well-defined project scope and objectives from the start. Clearly communicate the boundaries and deliverables to all stakeholders to manage expectations effectively.

9.3.2 Change Management:

Establishing a robust change management process to handle requested changes or scope adjustments. This process involves evaluating the impact of changes, obtaining stakeholder agreement, and updating project plans accordingly.

9.3.3 Prioritization and Trade-offs:

Balancing competing demands and priorities by making informed decisions about scope changes. This requires assessing the impact on project goals, timeline, and resources.

9.4 Effective Project Governance and Decision-Making:

Project governance and decision-making structures play a vital role in ensuring project success. Key considerations include:

9.4.1 Stakeholder Engagement:

Engaging relevant stakeholders throughout the project lifecycle and involving them in decision-making processes. This promotes transparency, accountability, and alignment with project goals.

9.4.2 Governance Framework:

Establishing a governance framework that defines roles, responsibilities, and decision-making authority. Clear governance structures ensure that decisions are made by the appropriate individuals or groups.

9.4.3 Decision-Making Criteria:

Defining decision-making criteria and guidelines to facilitate consistent and informed decision-making. This includes considering factors such as project objectives, risks, resource availability, and stakeholder input.

9.4.4 Monitoring and Review Mechanisms:

Implementing regular project reviews and checkpoints to assess project performance, compliance with governance standards, and the effectiveness of decision-making processes.

By monitoring progress, managing risks, utilizing agile project metrics and reporting, addressing scope creep, managing expectations, and establishing effective project governance and decision-making processes, project managers can effectively monitor and control WAgile projects, ensuring their successful completion.

Chapter 10: Scaling WAgile for Large Projects and Organizations

10.1 Challenges in Scaling WAgile:

Scaling Wagile practices to large projects and organizations presents unique challenges. This chapter explores common challenges and considerations when scaling Wagile. Key challenges include:

10.1.1 Complexity:

Large projects often involve multiple teams, dependencies, and complex workflows. Managing and coordinating these complexities requires a tailored approach that accounts for interdependencies and promotes effective collaboration.

10.1.2 Communication and Coordination:

Ensuring effective communication and coordination among distributed teams, stakeholders, and management becomes more challenging as projects and organizations scale. Clear communication channels, collaboration tools, and alignment mechanisms are necessary to maintain transparency and foster synergy.

10.1.3 Culture and Mindset:

Scaling WAgile practices requires a cultural shift across the organization. Aligning the mindset of individuals and teams with agile values, embracing collaboration, and encouraging continuous learning are essential for successful scaling.

10.2 Frameworks for Scaling Agile:

To address the challenges of scaling WAgile, various frameworks have been developed. This section highlights three popular frameworks:

10.2.1 SAFe (Scaled Agile Framework):

SAFe is a comprehensive framework designed to scale agile practices across large organizations. It provides guidance on portfolio management, value stream alignment, program execution, and team-level agile practices. SAFe emphasizes the synchronization of work, frequent feedback, and value delivery.

10.2.2 LeSS (Large-Scale Scrum):

LeSS is a framework that extends the principles and practices of Scrum to large-scale projects and organizations. It emphasizes simplicity, lean thinking, and cross-functional, self-organizing teams. LeSS encourages collaboration, transparency, and continuous improvement across the organization.

10.2.3 Nexus Framework:

The Nexus Framework is specifically designed for scaling Scrum. It provides guidance on how to organize and coordinate multiple Scrum teams working on the same product or project. The Nexus Framework emphasizes frequent integration, shared product backlog, and synchronized events to ensure effective collaboration and integration among teams.

10.3 Tailoring WAgile to Suit Organizational Needs:

While frameworks provide guidance, it is important to tailor the Wagile approach to suit the specific needs and context of the organization. Key considerations include:

10.3.1 Agile Transformation Strategy:

Developing a clear strategy and roadmap for scaling WAgile within the organization. This includes identifying areas for improvement, building agile capabilities, and gradually introducing Wagile practices across teams and departments.

10.3.2 Organizational Structure and Governance:

Aligning the organizational structure and governance with the principles of WAgile. This may involve restructuring teams, establishing cross-functional teams, and adjusting decision-making processes to facilitate collaboration and autonomy.

10.3.3 Training and Support:

Providing training and support to help teams and individuals understand and adopt WAgile practices. This includes agile coaching, mentoring, and providing resources to foster learning and skill development.

10.3.4 Continuous Improvement:

Encouraging a culture of continuous improvement and learning. This involves regularly reviewing and adjusting the scaled WAgile approach, incorporating feedback from teams and stakeholders, and refining processes to enhance efficiency and effectiveness.

10.3.5 Agile Tools and Technology:

Utilizing appropriate tools and technology to support collaboration, communication, and project management in a scaled WAgile environment. This may include agile project management software, collaborative platforms, and digital boards to facilitate remote collaboration and tracking.

By acknowledging the challenges, leveraging proven frameworks, and tailoring the WAgile approach to suit the organization's specific needs, large projects and organizations can successfully scale agile practices and achieve improved project outcomes and organizational agility.

Conclusion:

In this book, we have explored the concept of WAgile project management, a hybrid approach that combines the best of both Waterfall and Agile methodologies. WAgile offers a flexible and adaptive framework that allows organizations to strike a balance between structure and flexibility, enabling them to deliver successful projects in today's dynamic business environment.

Throughout the chapters, we have delved into various aspects of WAgile project management. We started by understanding the origins of WAgile and its key principles and values. We discussed the benefits and challenges of adopting WAgile, as well as guidelines for determining when to use this approach.

We then explored the WAgile project lifecycle, which encompasses initiation and project definition, planning and requirements gathering, iterative development and delivery, as well as project closure and evaluation. Each phase plays a crucial role in ensuring project success and delivering value to stakeholders.

Integrating Waterfall and Agile practices is another critical aspect of WAgile project management. We examined how detailed planning and documentation, sequential execution and phases, as well as predictive decision-making from the Waterfall approach, can be combined with Agile practices such as iterative development, cross-functional teams, and embracing change. By striking the right balance, organizations can harness the strengths of both methodologies and achieve improved project outcomes.

Managing stakeholder expectations is vital in any project, and WAgile is no exception. We explored strategies for identifying and engaging stakeholders, setting realistic expectations, establishing effective communication channels, and involving stakeholders throughout the project. By keeping stakeholders informed and engaged, organizations can build trust, manage risks, and ensure project success.

Agile planning is a core component of WAgile project management. We discussed techniques for defining project goals and objectives, using user stories and epics for planning, agile estimation and sizing, and release and iteration planning. By employing these techniques, organizations can create a flexible project schedule that adapts to changing requirements and optimizes value delivery.

Effective collaboration and cross-functional teams are crucial in WAgile. We explored strategies for building and managing cross-functional teams, facilitating collaboration and knowledge sharing, adopting agile leadership practices, and overcoming challenges in distributed teams. By fostering a collaborative environment, organizations can harness the collective expertise of their teams and drive project success.

Iterative development and delivery are key principles of WAgile. We discussed agile development practices, sprint planning and execution, measuring progress and tracking metrics, and ensuring continuous integration and quality assurance. By embracing iterative practices and continuously delivering value, organizations can respond to feedback, adapt to changing requirements, and maximize customer satisfaction.

Embracing change and continuous improvement is at the heart of WAgile project management. We explored strategies for adapting to changing requirements, implementing agile change management techniques, conducting retrospectives and lessons learned sessions, and cultivating a culture of continuous improvement. By embracing change as an opportunity for growth and fostering a learning culture, organizations can continuously enhance their project management practices and drive success.

Monitoring and controlling WAgile projects require tracking progress, managing risks, utilizing agile project metrics and reporting, addressing scope creep, and establishing effective project governance and decision-making processes. By employing these practices, organizations can maintain project visibility, make informed decisions, and ensure project objectives are met.

Finally, we discussed scaling WAgile for large projects and organizations. We examined the challenges in scaling, frameworks such as SAFe, LeSS, and the Nexus Framework, and the importance of tailoring the approach to suit organizational needs. By addressing challenges, leveraging frameworks, and tailoring the approach, organizations can successfully scale agile practices and achieve improved project outcomes and organizational agility.

In conclusion, WAgile project management offers a versatile and adaptive approach that combines the strengths of Waterfall and Agile methodologies. By embracing WAgile, organizations can navigate the complexities of today's business landscape, respond to change, deliver value to stakeholders, and achieve project success. With a solid understanding of the principles, practices, and frameworks discussed in this book, project managers and teams can embark on their WAgile journey with confidence and achieve remarkable results. Remember, WAgile is not a one-size-fits-all solution, but rather a mindset and approach that can be tailored to suit the unique needs of each organization. Embrace the principles, experiment, and continuously improve to unleash the full potential of WAgile project management.